GENIUS IDEAS
FOR
PLANETARY HEALING

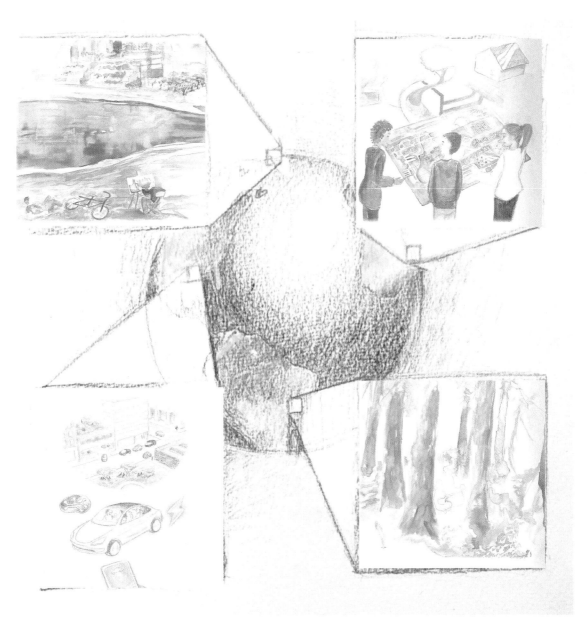

TOM CHI AND LUCILLE WHITAKER

Balboa Press books may be ordered through booksellers or by contacting:

Balboa Press
A Division of Hay House
1663 Liberty Drive
Bloomington, IN 47403
www.balboapress.com
844-682-1282

Because of the dynamic nature of the Internet, any web addresses or links contained in this book may have changed since publication and may no longer be valid. The views expressed in this work are solely those of the author and do not necessarily reflect the views of the publisher, and the publisher hereby disclaims any responsibility for them.

Any people depicted in stock imagery provided by Getty Images are models, and such images are being used for illustrative purposes only.
Certain stock imagery © Getty Images.

ISBN: 979-8-7652-2519-6 (sc)
979-8-7652-2518-9 (e)

Library of Congress Control Number: 2022903182

Print information available on the last page.

Balboa Press rev. date: 11/17/2022

BALBOA.PRESS
A DIVISION OF HAY HOUSE

TABLE OF CONTENTS

Introduction v

1. Understanding Earth Systems 1
    A. Seeing Our Earth from Space 2
    B. Natural Systems 4
    C. Our Earth's Climate 6
    D. Humanity's Influence 9

2. Agriculture 11
    A. The Future of Farming 12
    B. Soil Health 15
    C. Land Use 18

3. Energy & Fuels 20
    A. New Energy 21
    B. Transportation & Fuels 22
    C. Heat Energy 25

4. Materials 26
    A. Closing the Loop 27
    B. Viewing Our Cities 29
    C. Learning from Nature and Setting the Bounds 29

5. Environmental Restoration 33
    A. Forests 34
    B. Grasslands 36
    C. Wetlands 37
    D. Oceans 37
    E. Biodiversity 40

6. Reflection & Closing 41
    A. Seeking a Net Positive Future 41
    B. All Together 44
    C. Meditations for Planetary Healing 46

7. Further Reading: 47

INTRODUCTION

Since we wrote and illustrated the book *Our Prosperous Planet* over a decade ago we've been fortunate to witness and work with many teams applying genius ideas to planetary healing. Their work spans across growing food, soil health, ocean conservation, water systems, energy innovations, nature-based carbon capture, education, ethical fashion, packaging, cellular agriculture, plant-based foods, green building materials, smart buildings, community agriculture, self-driving electric cars and so much more. This book aims to present an overview of areas needing reinvention to create a world in harmony with natural processes as well as discuss current developments and inspired innovations that are leading the way. We invite you to explore ideas with us that reinvent, reimagine, and regenerate with the revival of the natural world in mind. One of our main goals in sharing inspiring developments toward a regenerative economy is the hope that we inspire brilliant new ideas to improve and enrich our lives and our overall planetary health.

We are all members of a handful of generations with the rare opportunity and responsibility to set a new course. This new course can include saving endangered species and enhancing the quality of life for all while simultaneously protecting and regenerating our beautiful, shared planet. If we don't rise to the challenge, we may be facing a degraded planet for thousands of years. So, let's take a deep look at some of the recent events in history that pushed us to dedicate our time and studies in the direction of sustainability.

In the early 20th century, we were a world at war that was rapidly industrializing based on fossil fuel consumption. This trajectory has now diverged too substantially from what the atmosphere, hydrosphere, and biosphere can support. Now, in the 21st century, the internet has democratized communication to the level where for the first time we can become one global civilization. This is happening at exactly the moment we must come together to make wise and effective choices for the shared prosperity of all of life on Earth. Ours is an amazing time in history, where we must grow our consciousness and understanding of our Earth much more quickly than we further propagate our damaging practices. Through generations of invention, scientific inquiry, cultural progression, and commerce we have become a species with the ability to create (or destroy) at a scale that affects all of life on the planet. This book seeks to build our shared understanding so we can be conscious in our collective creation and move toward the long-term health of life on this planet.

This will be a journey with many steps, and the truth is that we are still learning how to play this role. There is no one with all the answers to tell us exactly how we will make this happen, a reality that is both exciting and challenging. This is why we are excited to share – because we need *your* creativity and the efforts of so many people, communities, cities, and beyond to realize this future together.

1. UNDERSTANDING EARTH SYSTEMS

If we can better understand what healthy natural systems look like, we can create a foundation for realigning our economic and civic systems toward a world where humanity is a net positive to nature. Just as nature provides so many things that are useful for us to thrive on so many levels, we must also give back useful things, if you will, for nature to thrive so it can continue to support us and all life on Earth. When we stop to notice, we see that every few seconds, we breathe in and we breathe out, in an ongoing cycle that supports the essential processes that keep us alive. Plants also breathe in and breathe out, in an ongoing cycle that mirrors ours, and these two intertwined respiratory cycles support all of plant and animal life on the planet. Life on this planet is an intricate interlocking cascade of such timeless cycles, governing the interplay of air, water, nutrients, and energy. When we nourish these cycles to nourish ourselves, both the planet and people benefit. When we work against these cycles – by halting or truncating them to siphon off resources for our needs alone, quite quickly less is available for all. It's important to take time away from our screens and the bustle of daily routine to simply pause sometimes, spend time in nature, and connect with gratitude to the miracle of life. From that foundation we can better explore how we intend to be good stewards of these gifts. Such reflections are how this book came to be and the combination of the lessons that nature holds with the genius ideas that we pursue as a society can create the path to planetary healing.

So let us start by listening and better understanding the cycles that drive the health and function of our world. Then we can imagine ways to participate in their bounty while strengthening their health and function. The simple shift from looking at everything around us as "resources" toward a viewpoint where we are all contributors to the interconnected cycle of life, helps to make clear how investing in the health of natural cycles might create more "resources" (or create them with better resilience and longevity) than a short-term extractive mindset. Let us move forward in generosity and foresight with each generation leaving more for the one after it - more wisdom, more topsoil, more ecosystem health and resilience, and more capability to care for each other and all of life.

ʌ. SEEING OUR EARTH FROM SPACE

From space, it is clear that the Earth is physically finite. There are only so many tons of each element, only so many water molecules to fill our rivers, skies, and oceans, only so much surface area for life to stretch across. Yet over the course of billions of years, the planet has been progressively enriched. Not by the introduction of more stuff, but by the brilliance of life and its ability to metabolize, organize, and express that finite stuff into countless new patterns that support even more life. Our same planet, which just 1 billion years ago only held single-celled life,[1] has supported the emergence of nearly unimaginable diversity and possibility, ranging from plants which harvest and store energy that foundationally drive our ecosystems, to fungi which create vast communication networks between species and help to recycle nutrients, to animals that swim, run, and fly across the myriad terrains of our planet. And, of course, this includes our own species, which has developed the ability to reflect, record, reason, and build upon our knowledge, abilities, and relationships with each generation. Our hope is that the topics shared in this book inspire creative ideas that help us envision a better world for all. We are truly hopeful that humanity as a whole will turn toward the light and see all life as the miracle that it is. By consciously thinking about how our breath oxygenates us will not only help our breathing, overall health and well-being, it will inspire us to go for walks, open a window, bring nature indoors for healthier living spaces, and most importantly appreciate it, regenerate, and reenvision what it means to live in harmony with the natural world.

It's time for us to make the decision to continue with the greater arc of life on this planet. To have our presence be a force that enables even more expression, diversity, and thriving. We are kin with organisms that are working with the same basic goal: to savor of every photon toward the maximization of diverse nutrient flows. Or as Janine Beynus would say: "life creates the conditions for life." We savor photons because they are the source of energy that drives everything around us. We maximize diverse nutrient flows because the more sophisticated and nuanced the flows, the richer and healthier the ecosystem. We can become a society that consciously maximizes diverse nutrient flows to enrich our own lives while continuous expanding the capacity for nature to thrive. Such an effort would put us in alignment with what life on this planet has been contributing to since the very first single-celled organisms. Simple principles like this can result in the profound beauty of coral reef, an alpine forest, or an orchid pollinated by a hummingbird. Our own civilization can mirror this level of nuance and beauty by investing in the processes that maximize diverse nutrient flows. With care and focus, we will move away from the ceaseless extraction of resources and toward an economy that centers around investment in the metabolic processes that create natural wealth. In doing so we build the engine of abundance and participate in it, as opposed to removing abundance and degrading the processes that create it. In the process we will not only make it possible for the human story on this planet to be a lasting one, but also, we will shift our role from exploitation toward one of growing understanding, care, and joyful coexistence with Earth's species.

This image illustrates some of the global satellites that currently monitor the health of our planet. These satellites can become our guides for how our planet is changing and help to guide the process of repair and regeneration. Each community also has a big role. When even a few members of a community are familiar with what local ecosystem health looks like, it provides early recognition of damage and a template for care and rehabilitation.

---

[1] https://www.newscientist.com/article/dn17453-timeline-the-evolution-of-life/

B. NATURAL SYSTEMS

Hydrological, Nutrients, Energy

With the exception of some geothermal/tectonic processes, the sun powers all essential cycles we experience on the Earth's surface. It evaporates water, which becomes the rain and snow that animate the hydrological cycle. It powers photosynthesis, driving energy storage and nutrient availability throughout the food web. Through differential warming, it drives the winds and ocean currents. Together these processes support the movement of energy and nutrients that support all life we know. Our goal as a species must be to move towards understanding, caring for, and amplifying the life-supporting abilities of these cycles. We now have the ability to measure the flow of atmospheric, surface and ground hydrology and can be skillful in the design of our economic systems to ensure the long-term health of these flows are cared for. In the same way that a useful invention made of some well-organized materials can provide more services for less money to more people, improvements to how we as a society work with air, water, soil, and biodiversity can provide more services to life for less energy and effort going forward. As an example of this practice, the early Hawaiians organized the land into Moku and Ahupua'a.[2] These were pie-shaped slices of land running from a point on the mountaintop and fanning out to the shoreline. They were defined by how water flowed on the land and aimed to be a coherent slice of watershed. Given this way of dividing land for care, there was no such thing as someone upstream polluting a downstream community - by design of the slice - it would be the same party causing and experiencing both. This gave each local community a profound understanding of the healthy flow of water across the land and both simplified and made clear the responsibility to support this healthy flow. The net result was that the community could manage the land in a way that savored the flow of healthy water and enriched both the populace and diverse ecosystems at each elevation in the journey of that water.

---

[2] https://www.youtube.com/watch?v=Pl87WjChPpw

Similar to a watershed, we can understand the flow of nutrients as its own type of watershed. The way that life works with nutrients is to draw them from the air (nitrogen, carbon, oxygen), and from the soil (nitrogen, phosphorus, potassium, sulfur, magnesium, calcium, plus various micronutrients), first to support the immediate needs of specific organism, and subsequently making those nutrients available to other organisms via the food or decomposition chains. Given time in any location, life will make more nutrients bioavailable in an ecosystem, thus making it easier for more life to flourish with less effort. We have the ability to do the same as we build our food and industrial systems, as they too draw on many of the same raw materials. If we do this with an awareness of the nutrient-shed, we prevent our systems from causing harm through accidental drought or glut of nutrients. Systems that last cannot be wasteful in these ways.

At the largest scale, we might do well to understand the plants and air as the respiratory system of the Earth, the soil as the digestive system, and the waters as the circulatory system. A homeostatic balance of flows is what keeps us personally alive, and so too a homeostatic balance of air, water, soil keeps the entire planet alive. Stopping the flow or severely imbalancing it can lead to long term (and sometimes acute) degradation of health. Investment in the vibrant health of these flows means more abundance and easier support of life worldwide. It is the practice of investing in the flows (aka the verbs of nature) that create our natural resources instead of "investing" to exploit the resources (aka the nouns of nature) which is the fundamental shift in orientation we need. While it may seem more economical to just extract the nouns for profit, there is tremendously more leverage in investing in the verbs and sharing in the nouns that such flows create. At the small scale, companies can invest in the natural flows (or in protecting the natural flows) that feed their core inputs. At the national scale, protecting these flows are in fact good for business. We can incentivize businesses to develop ongoing improvements in tending these flows as well as ever less-damaging ways of sharing in their bounty. The businesses that perform better on these metrics can be allotted more access than those who have more destructive practices.

C. OUR EARTH'S CLIMATE

Carbon Emission -Greenhouse Gases (GHG)

Through the use of oil, gas, and coal we are making use of energy captured by ancient life - most of it alive during the Paleozoic (541 to 252 million years ago) and Mesozoic (252 to 66 million years ago) eras. In other words, we are taking the energy stored over hundreds of millions of years and putting it to use over the course of just a few hundred years (roughly a million times faster than it took to store). While the planet has experienced significant changes in climate over the millennia, these typically take place over tens of thousands to millions of years. By using this energy stored over hundreds of millions of years in a short time period, we have emitted trillions of tons of CO_2, increasing the level of CO_2 in the atmosphere by roughly 50% over pre-industrial levels at the time of this writing. This has led to large scale climate destabilization which will continue as long as this imbalance remains. We are already seeing substantial disruptions in the form of destabilized temperatures, rainfall and ice cover. In Earth's history, when changes like these occur in a short span, they have driven mass extinctions. All evidence points to our current actions doing exactly that – it's estimated that we are extincting species at roughly 1000x the base rate[3] (the fossil record shows a pace of roughly 0.1-1 species going extinct per million species per year), and unless we foundationally change our approach to how we power our civilization, half of all species face extinction by the year 2100.[4] Now more than ever we need genius ideas and solutions that help us stop and reverse this tragedy. We have hope in humankind and our ability to heal. Planetary healing is possible if we put our minds and hearts together to find healthier ways of doing things.

At the moment, we are continuing a 150-year practice of pulling from vast stores of oil, gas and coal beneath the earth's surface and burning it to produce power. The total amount of carbon in fossil deposits is more than 10x what is held in the atmosphere. Burning even ⅕ of that would render the planet uninhabitable to life as we know it, so there is no situation where we can use the "proven reserves" currently claimed by fossil fuel companies without experiencing a mass extinction of everything (including ourselves). We have currently burned about 2.2 trillion tons, of which 650 billion have been absorbed by the land, 550 billion have been absorbed by the ocean (increasing the acidity of global oceans by 30%),[5] and 1 trillion tons are in the atmosphere, destabilizing our climate. Herein lies the first area of challenge/opportunity -- finding new ways of generating power for our buildings, industry, and transportation, as well as new ways of growing food - all of which we will discuss throughout this book. Let's reimagine how we impact the climate by consciously inventing new technologies and deploying approaches that not only mitigate and eliminate but also reverse climate destabilization.

[3] 10.1126/science.1246752
[4] https://www.zmescience.com/ecology/world-problems/world-species-extinction-27022017/
[5] https://www.pmel.noaa.gov/co2/story/What+is+Ocean+Acidification%3F

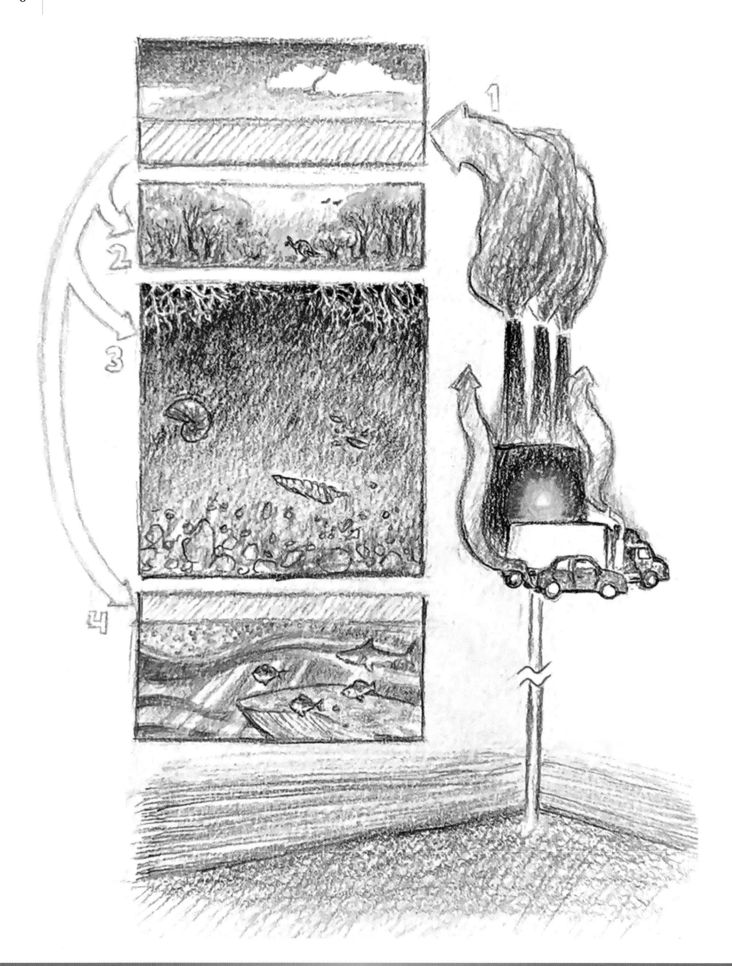

Other Greenhouse Gases (GHGs)

In addition to carbon emissions, which represent 76% of global emissions (65% from industry, 11% from land use changes)[6] there are a few other gases that are significantly affecting the atmosphere and driving destabilization of the systems that keep this planet alive. They include:

- Methane (16%) - A far more potent gas for atmospheric warming in the short term, we generate it via soil management practices, livestock, and leaking natural gas infrastructure. Changes to land use can also release methane, for example draining wetlands or melting permafrost both accelerate decay of organic matter and drive additional methane emissions.

- Nitrous Oxide (6%) - Largely generated from our present-day, fertilizer-intensive approach to agriculture, as well as from livestock and human waste. To address it, we need to create a healthier relationship to the nutrient cycle by applying less fertilizer and instead closing the nutrient loop through healthier soil function from the activity of plants, animals, fungi, and beneficial microbes on the land.

- F-gases (2%) - These are extremely long-lived in the atmosphere and are hundreds to thousands of times more potent than CO2. In the long run, if we don't curb their use, they will make up a larger and larger percentage of greenhouse gases because they can take thousands to 100,000 years to cycle out of the atmosphere. Presently, the main source of F-gas emission is air conditioning and cooling, where they are used as refrigerants (used to run the cooling cycle because of their lower boiling point).

D. HUMANITY'S INFLUENCE

Pollution

Beyond GHGs and their destabilizing influence on the atmosphere, we also do damage via pollution - be it toxic chemistry, plastic waste, disruptive materials concentrations, and even noise pollution. Pollution starts with what materials we choose to employ in manufacturing in the first place. When creating a product or service that will be widely distributed (packaging, for example), we should strive to use Earth-compatible materials – defined as materials having a simple pathway for nature to return it to a form useful for life. When creating products or services that require rarer materials or non-Earth-compatible chemistry, the manufacturer and/or brand must actively design ways to close the material loop so as to prevent loss of these materials to the environment. The development of new, low-cost, Earth compatible materials and low-cost reverse logistic supply chains for non-compatible materials, as well as thoughtful end-of-life considerations during the design process are all essential for attacking pollution at the root. In the interim, while we are developing these capabilities, we will need to be skillful in the capture and appropriate handling of municipal and industrial wastes.

---

[6] https://www.epa.gov/ghgemissions/global-greenhouse-gas-emissions-data

Land-Use Changes

We make some of our largest negative impacts to the planet by how we clear and use land, whether it be from soil-degrading agriculture, mining, wetland draining, real estate development, or physical infrastructure that splits ecosystems and disrupts migration pathways. Land use changes that also include increased demand on water can have a large accidental footprint by altering the downstream availability of water to ecosystems hundreds of miles away. When we alter land for human purposes, we can look to ensure that the processes that build the soils and distribute the waters are fully supported or even beneficially expanded by the changes we make. One could imagine governments having as part of the licensing and auction process a requirement to have companies compete on how substantially they could support and expand the ecosystem services of an area as a result of their operations. This type of innovation is no harder than any other.

Biodiversity Loss

Every species, in its presence, behavior, and foundational genetic makeup, represents a unique way of being and set of solutions for living in the ecosystem and microclimate from which it comes. One could think of its DNA like a book upon which is written the accumulated wisdom of how a being can thrive in a specific setting. As we lose a species, it is akin to losing the wisdom of that book, and losing the beauty and ingenuity of that way of being. At this juncture in history we are driving a rate of global extinction which is roughly 1000x faster than the base rate. The pace is so fast, the books are being burned faster than we can even open them. It is like the Library of Alexandria burning down every day as the wisdom of these forms of life turn to dust. Most of the species lost have not been deeply studied, and through their loss, we may have missed out on the cure for deadly diseases, the clever design solutions built into their physical form, or what company they might have been to their kin in the ecosystem. As we shift to more harmonious ways of being, we can consciously work to bring extinction back down to the base rate, and in the interim, we can massively expand our efforts to study, understand, and be amidst these species so we can better invest in what will support their long-term health.

2. AGRICULTURE

Agriculture has a unique role because it is the way that humanity can work consciously with photosynthesis - the foundational process that stores solar energy and drives the food web above ground, in the soil, and in the seas. Agriculture is one of the least expensive ways to deploy one of the most sophisticated technologies we've encountered: the seed. An integrative approach to agriculture can serve the nutritional and cultural needs of each community while supporting habitat and soil regeneration. Through what we grow we can actively improve the fertility of soil and thereby enrich our present-day livelihoods as well as future communities. The industrial farming model we have applied widely in richer nations has focused on a narrow definition of productivity which maximizes single crop yields at the expense of soil and long term ecosystem and human health. While this has worked in some capacities, it does long term damage to the land and is not ideal to export to developing nations or even continue in developed nations. We are at a juncture where there is much work to do to make agriculture ecologically sound, nutritionally complete, and just.

A. THE FUTURE OF FARMING

We are entering an era where climate destabilization is going to challenge the ways we have been growing. Over the next 30 years, we will need to feed 2 billion more people with 300 million fewer people living in rural areas.[7] Given this, we must learn to produce food more reliably, at larger scales, on less land, with fewer farmers. Here are some growing practices that can help meet the need:

- **Controlled environment agriculture** - Intensive greenhouse agriculture that is partially or fully automated will allow us to grow at much lower costs. Such systems can yield several growing seasons in a year, independent of outdoor temperatures making a variety of healthy foods available year-round. They can also grow using 90% less water, 80% less fertilizer input, and little to no herbicide, fungicide, and pesticides. Such systems are most economically competitive if they grow via sunlight, not grow lights, although grow lights can work for a handful of high value / kg products.
- **Precision agriculture** - Is a term used to describe a collection of techniques where growing is managed carefully with technology. This includes techniques like drip irrigation programmed to deliver precise amounts of water and nutrients to plant roots, as well as tools like drones and tractors outfitted with the ability to sense field conditions and take specific actions like input application, weed management, or selective harvesting.
- **Regenerative intercropping, agroecology** - In environments where labor is lower cost, and local communities need a broad range of nutritious and marketable produce to meet food needs and lift them up economically, regenerative intercropping provides a way to grow a lot of food on small plots while enriching soils and limiting biodiversity loss. The ethos of this work is to make farming more productive by growing a whole ecosystem including beneficial insects, co-supportive plants, and soil microbes.
- **Agroforestry** - This is similar to regenerative intercropping, but uses a variety of trees as the foundation of the planting plan. This recognizes that different plants have evolved to grow at different layers from canopy to understory to forest floor, and has the added benefit of providing building materials, fuel, shade, and further stabilizing the land against extreme weather. Because these techniques provide so many co-benefits they can be a boon to communities that are looking to build local resilience and sufficiency.

While there are so many exciting developments in the future of farming, there is also much to learn from indigenous agricultural practices. Some of these practices are portable, such as "the three sisters" technique where squash, corn, and beans are planted together to help each other survive and thrive.[8] Other practices are deeply situated in place, such as mesquite dryland restoration, to take best advantage of what a landscape offers and limits. These long-lived techniques along with the modern practices above, all represent tools and technology that if used appropriately can help support harmony and bounty from the land. As we grow, we will move beyond agriculture simply as a means of maximizing monocrop production into an agriculture as an endeavor that can nourish individuals, ecosystems, soils, communities, and future generations. This industry, which currently drives the largest-scale ecosystem destruction can become the industry that drives robust health, from root-tip to treetop and every organism in between.

---

[7] https://ourworldindata.org/grapher/urban-and-rural-population-2050?country=~OWID_WRL
[8] https://en.wikipedia.org/wiki/Three_Sisters_(agriculture)

Future of Meats and Proteins:

We currently use roughly half of the habitable land on the Earth to produce our food and 77% of that is used for meat production via a mix of grazing livestock and using cropland to grow feed, providing just 18% of our food calories.[9] It's essential for us to produce meat and proteins in a way that is harmonious with the cycles of the planet and the following techniques coming into wider practice could support such a shift:

- **Plant-based meat alternatives** - we are learning to match the flavor of many animal-based foods with plant-based alternatives that are far less resource-intensive for the planet. Recent developments have enabled plant-based meats to brown and cook in a manner similar to traditional meat, further reducing the gap between the two experiences. Our efforts to work with plant-based ingredients in new ways will ultimately expand the universe of flavors we can experience. At the current moment, some of the constituent plants (e.g. soy) contribute to land use change and environmental impacts in their own right, but on a whole, if they displace meat calories, they still reduce the net ecological load. As plant-based alternatives are made from more regeneratively grown ingredients, we can offer more foods that actively heal the planet.

- **Cellular agriculture** - refers to the use of cells to produce our food. This may range from using familiar organisms like yeast to create protein all the way to the newer practice of growing animal products starting with animal cells. For example, starting with a small collection of cow cells and having them multiply to create a meatball or hamburger. To get a sense of how these efforts may help the planet, it takes around 23 calories of energy to produce 1 calorie of beef via current factory farming methods. Using cellular agriculture, it could take as little as 3 calories of energy input to produce 1 calorie of beef as you are only feeding the cells, not tending a whole animal throughout its life.

- **Intensive Rotational Grazing** - While the previous two techniques all point toward a world with fewer livestock, historically, soil has been built in concert with both plants and animals on the land. Given this, even as we successfully reduce the total amount of livestock needed to feed us, for the livestock we continue to keep, we may choose to transition our grazing practices to intensive rotational grazing to help enrich soils and restore landscapes. This works by having the animals on the move in tight herds, never grazing for more than a day or two in a specific plot. This provides enough time for the animals to break up hardened soils with their hooves and fertilize the land via their manure, but not long enough to graze down the vegetation severely. The net result is a recharged soil microbiome, deeper root development, and substantially increased soil organic carbon.

---

[9] https://ourworldindata.org/land-use

INTENSIVE
ROTATIONAL
GRAZING

B. SOIL HEALTH

Soil carbon sequestration

Soil has the ability to store tremendous amounts of carbon.[10] Just as a healthy ecosystem above ground represents a long-term carbon store, a healthy soil ecosystem below ground can contribute massively to carbon storage. In this book we outline a number of soil regenerative practices, including rotational grazing and soil regenerative agriculture. It's estimated that within the top meter of soils around the world store, the planet already stores 3x more carbon than the total carbon in the atmosphere, and 10x more than the current overage of CO_2 in the atmosphere. This means it would only take a global increase in soil carbon of 11% to address our current (2022) excess of atmospheric CO_2 of 1 trillion tons. Local and National governments are now looking at programs that can help to incentivize the agricultural and land management activities that encourage this form of natural carbon capture. In a number of subsistence and developing world contexts, moving to soil regenerative practices can happen directly as industrial agriculture has not yet taken hold.

---

[10] http://www.fao.org/soils-portal/soil-management/soil-carbon-sequestration/en/

While healthy soils sequester far more carbon, building healthy soil also has numerous co-benefits ranging from erosion control, to water table recharge, to improved resilience in the face of adverse weather.[11] On top of these structural benefits, healthy soil has the economic benefit of lowering the cost of growing. Farms with healthy soil fare better in flood and drought, require substantially less fertilizers and pesticides, and are more efficient at drawing nutrients from the soil as well as liberating new nutrients from the underlying substrate or fixing them from the atmosphere.

To best care for soil, it is helpful to understand how healthy soil works.
1) The energy that allows soils to function comes from the sun. As sunlight hits green plants it drives photosynthesis - a process which takes carbon dioxide from the air and combines it with water to make food for the plant and store energy.
2) The energy is stored as simple plant sugars, that then travel throughout the plant to support its growth. The plant sugars that go down to the roots have a special role to play.
3) Beyond contributing to root growth, they can be passed on to a vast network of organisms via mycorrhizal networks. This transfer of plant sugars from green plants is the primary engine providing the energy to power soil life.
4) The mycorrhiza broker an exchange - in order to get access to the plant sugars, then will tap into distant nutrient resources containing nutrients that the plants need. As these plant sugars go beyond the roots into the larger soil system, they feed the entire underground ecosystem, either directly through relationship to the mycorrhizal hyphae, or via the materials leftover in decaying organisms.

Soil health and human health are deeply intertwined. As we learn to care for soils, we learn that our own health improves. It's been recently discovered that soil contains natural antidepressants. It's been studied and tested. The microbes in soil called *Mycobacterium vaccae* were discovered to mirror the effect on neurons that prescription antidepressants provide.[12] The bacterium is found in soil and can stimulate serotonin in the brain, which boosts mood and relaxation.[13] The way it works is that these tiny miraculous antidepressant microbes in soil cause our cytokine levels (proteins in the body also responsible for stronger immune responses)[14] to rise, which results in the production of higher levels of serotonin in the brain.[15] and that process can support improved mental health, overall happiness and well-being.

Given this, it is no surprise that gardening is a mood lifter to so many who practice it. So next time you need a mood boost, consider a small gardening project or just going to a natural place where the soil is breathing. Perhaps join a community garden or volunteer at a native plant nursery to help with ecosystem restoration. There are so many brilliant ways nature heals us and it's fun to get involved, learn and share how to keep ourselves and the soil around us healthy.

---

[11] https://food.berkeley.edu/wp-content/uploads/2016/05/GSPPCarbon_03052016_FINAL.pdf

[12] http://www.sage.edu/newsevents/news/?story_id=240785 Mind & Brain/Depression and Happiness – Raw Data *"Is Dirt the New Prozac?" by Josie Glausiusz, Discover Magazine:* https://discovermagazine.com/2007/jul/raw-data-is-dirt-the-new-prozac

[13] https://www.gardeningknowhow.com/garden-how-to/soil-fertilizers/antidepressant-microbes-soil.htm

[14] https://en.wikipedia.org/wiki/Cytokine

[15] *Identification of an Immune-Responsive Mesolimbocortical Serotonergic System: Potential Role in Regulation of Emotional Behavior," by Christopher Lowry et al.:* https://www.ncbi.nlm.nih.gov/pmc/articles/PMC1868963/

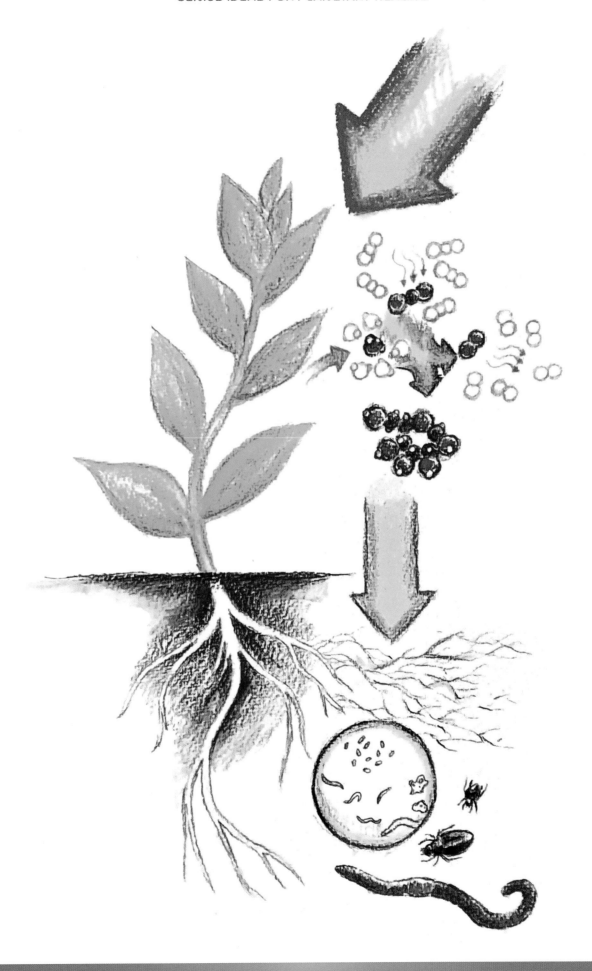

C. LAND USE

The Earth has a finite surface area of 510 million km² / 197 million mi². 71% of the Earth is covered with ocean. Of the 29% that is land (149 million km² / 57.5 million mi²), roughly 30% of it is near uninhabitable landscapes in the form of vast desert or ice sheets. Of the 70% of land which is habitable (104 million km² / 40.3 million mi²), we use roughly *half* (51 million km² / 19.7 million mi²) to grow our food between cropland and pastureland.[16] As the human population grows toward 10 billion this century and as per capita consumption increases, the expanding need for food production has the potential to destroy the last refuges of biodiversity on Earth. Currently, the Amazonian, Indonesian, and Malaysian rainforests are being destroyed for soy and palm oil agriculture. While this is an outcome that few would directly support, a large interconnected web of commerce makes us all contributors to this destruction. In the case of the Amazon, 80% of the soy grown there is fed to cattle and other livestock. In other words, our desire for animal protein in our diets connected with our feed practices which aims for large scale "efficient" production results in these collective outcomes. With palm oil, it is our demand for snack foods, cleaning products, and cooking oil which is driving the destruction.[17] The good news is that our personal decisions help to shape these markets, and supporting more sustainable practices for these products or switching to alternatives that have lesser ecological impact is something available to us all. There are also entrepreneurs, scientists, and engineers working to create better protein and palm oil alternatives which we can look to support.

A tiny sliver, roughly 1% of Earth's total land surface is covered directly by freshwater, and similarly, roughly 1% is covered by the human-built environment. While smaller in physical extent, both can have a tremendous impact on the lands they connect with. The built environment often has the majority of its impact from the use of water. Globally, 70% of freshwater used by humans is directed toward agriculture, which is draining water tables and freshwater lakes. We also divert or dam rivers, pollute waters with industrial chemistry, pollute with mining wastes, etc. We also have a habit of draining wetlands (which would otherwise help to process our wastes) and modify coastlines for real estate potential.

Between using half of the habitable land for agriculture and redirecting water sources to that agriculture, we are having a massive negative impact through our land use. The many paths forward mentioned in this chapter represent material shifts that could dramatically reduce land use, water use, sequester carbon, grow healthier food, support local communities, create habitat, and improve our resilience to extreme weather. Upgrading our agricultural system to create minimum impact proteins and positive impact crops is one of the most important moves we must make as a civilization. Additionally we can volunteer to help protect endangered lands. For example, perhaps start by joining and donating to organizations such *Rainforest Trust, Rainforest Action Network,* and *Earth Alliance*[18] working to *"address the urgent threats to our planet's life support systems, including a growing climate crisis and staggering loss of biodiversity"*, as well as *Re:wild* making strides to heal the planet with the mission to *"protect and restore the diversity of life on Earth"*.[19]

---

[16] https://ourworldindata.org/land-use
[17] https://www.treehugger.com/sneaky-names-palm-oil-4858743
[18] https://ealliance.org/
[19] rewild.org

3. ENERGY & FUELS

One way to understand the energy we use is to compare it to the amount of energy used by the human body. The human body uses around 100 watts - this is the energy that powers all your cells, allows you to move, think, and maintain your body temperature. In terms of energy consumption beyond the body, worldwide average energy use is 79 million btu / person = 83 billion joules.[20] A watt is a joule/second, so given 3.154e8 seconds in a year, this comes out to 264 watts. So we could say that on average, each person on Earth is using the energy of 2.6 people. Of course, this is not evenly distributed. America does 309 million btu / person - year = 326e9 / 3.154e8 = 1033 watts, or about 10 people worth of help from our energy using appliances.

While it may seem intrinsically unsustainable for humans to use energy beyond what the body needs, the potential for damage comes from the style of use. For example, when a bee interacts with a flower, it is benefiting from a significant amount of energy beyond its immediate body. Bees gather so much extra energy that they have sufficient energy to store in the form of honey. When it comes to the style, while the bee is "taking" energy from the flower, it is doing so in a way that supports the long-term flourishing of the flower and the larger ecosystem. The human style of energy extraction and storage leaves much to be desired compared to this approach. As we deepen our understanding of ways to work with the vast energy in the natural world, we can move toward an approach that is as supportive to our world as the bee is to the flower. Let's imagine new ideas to create our built environment with all of this in mind.

While electricity generation has attracted a lot of the headlines, it only represents about one quarter (25%) of our net emissions. Roughly another quarter (26%) comes from agriculture and forestry practices, 21% comes from industrial heat, 14% from transportation fuels, and 6% from buildings.[21] This means 3/4ths of the emissions problem will remain even if we move to 100% renewable electricity generation. Given this, the full menu of what we will need in the next two decades looks more like:

- 100% renewable electricity generation + grid storage & transmission infrastructure
- Negative emission agriculture (via a focus on soil health)
- Low or no-emission approaches to industrial process heat
- Full electrification of ground transportation, low net emission fuels for ship and air
- Efficient HVAC using Low-GHG refrigerants, heat pumps, thermal storage, and LED lighting for buildings
- Additional carbon sequestration and cycling from restoring forests, grasslands, and wetlands

Let's dig in a step into some of these changes.

---

[20] https://www.eia.gov/tools/faqs/faq.php?id=85
[21] https://www.epa.gov/sites/default/files/2016-05/global_emissions_sector_2015.png

A. NEW ENERGY

Renewable Generation

Most of our energy is still being generated via coal, oil and gas. Wind and solar have become directly cost competitive[22] for cost of generation (less than 5 cents per kWh)[23] in most of the world, while hydroelectric, geothermal, and nuclear still have to be very specifically sited. Depending on where we generate and when we use energy, there are two additional considerations:

1) **Transmission costs** - Creating large wind and solar installations has benefits in terms of dollar per generated kW, but if installations are far away from the populations or industries using the power, then transmission costs can rival generation costs, roughly doubling the costs. National or regional infrastructure investments can help bring this cost down substantially. Outside of large infrastructure, closer siting of generation and use intrinsically brings down transmission costs, the shortest form would be rooftop solar, or a local wind/solar generation site that powers a community microgrid or specific industrial facility.

2) **Storage** - Since wind and sun energy are not available at every minute of the day and since power is not used evenly throughout a day, there will always be some level of mismatch between how much power is being generated and how much is being consumed. Broadly, energy storage is a way of balancing out the variations in supply and demand over time. This could take the forms ranging from a small electric or thermal battery in the home on the order of 10kWh all the way up to grid scale storage in the 10GWh range.[24] At the moment, most large-scale grid storage comes in the form of hydroelectric dams and pumped storage. While this has huge carrying capacity, it must be very specifically sited (meaning there are very specific places where it can work). A number of companies are looking at chemical batteries, flow batteries, molten salt and mechanical storage as means to store energy at various scales, and these technologies while more expensive than pumped storage, should work in a much wider range of settings.

With more transmission lines and more flexible grid storage it gets progressively easier to scale up inexpensive renewable generation and experience the full benefit of those cost savings. Much of this century will be centered around the transition of electricity generation to these sources.

Baseload

It can be helpful for a grid to have a level of power that is always available, as it both reduces the total amount of overcapacity that would need to be built to address the variability of renewable sources, and it provides a foundation for the rare time periods when all variable generating renewable sources are at a low generation ebb. Hydroelectric power is currently the largest source of baseload

---

[22] https://en.wikipedia.org/wiki/Levelized_cost_of_energy
[23] https://energypost.eu/5-charts-show-the-rapid-fall-in-costs-of-renewable-energy/
[24] https://en.wikipedia.org/wiki/Bath_County_Pumped_Storage_Station

and renewable generation in the world, clocking in at 16% of the world's electricity generation.[25] While substantial it does come at an ecological cost of disrupting surface hydrology and interrupting migration paths. Next is nuclear, which provides about 10% of global electricity from 440 operating reactors.[26] While nuclear was marketed under the idea of being "too cheap to meter," it currently costs more than renewable generation, so while there may not be a strong incentive to massively increase nuclear generation, existing plants make sense to continue running to provide baseload while the larger generation transition happens. Beyond these, the remainder of current baseload comes from fossil fuel sources – coal, natural gas, and oil (on some island nations). Of these options, natural gas peaker plants are the least expensive to run and have relatively fast ramp up / ramp down times compared to coal and oil. Those are the economics to beat with renewable no/low-emission replacements.

B. TRANSPORTATION & FUELS

The unique challenge of transportation fuels is they need to be carried along with the vehicle. This means that two attributes, the energy density per kilogram and the energy density per volume become important considerations that define what fuels can work in which vehicles. If the energy density per kilogram is too low, it means the vehicle will need to carry more weight to move. If the energy density per volume is too low, then the vehicle will need to be larger to accommodate storing its fuel. Both of these attributes lead to lower fuel efficiency, the first because of weight, the second because of drag. When it comes to cargo vehicles, deficiencies here also become a problem as it uses up space that would otherwise go to commercial payload.

Lithium batteries have recently emerged as the choice power source for electric cars and light trucks. While these batteries have roughly 1/100th the energy density of gasoline, the extra weight of the battery is somewhat offset by weight and space savings from a substantially simplified drivetrain - down from over 200 moving parts in an internal combustion car to around 17 moving parts for an electric car.[27] This bodes well for downshifting our use of oil over time, as 75% of oil usage goes to fuels for road vehicles,[28] but there remain significant challenges for decarbonizing flights and ocean freight. Flights are challenged by both energy density metrics, as a heavier plane with more drag is not going to fare well compared to current models. Given this, the most likely approach to decarbonize flying would be to electrify short haul flights (<1.5 hours) and use biofuels or fuel from pyrolyzed plastic for long haul flights. Both of these approaches are likely to require subsidies as they are more expensive than pumping new oil. Hydrogen is another possibility, as it has more than 3x the energy density / kg of jet fuel, but there is substantial development still to go to integrate these systems into aircraft.

[25] https://www.nationalgeographic.com/environment/article/hydropower
[26] https://www.iea.org/reports/nuclear-power-in-a-clean-energy-system
[27] https://www.nrdc.org/experts/madhur-boloor/electric-vehicles-101
[28] https://www.eia.gov/outlooks/ieo/pdf/transportation.pdf

Electrification and Automation. Two big changes are happening to vehicles - the move toward electrification and the development of self-driving technology. Together they create the possibility of dramatically shrinking both the individual carbon impact of each car as well as the total number of cars needed to cover our transportation needs. Electric cars are emissions free in that they don't have a tailpipe or any combustion of fossil fuels in their engines. That said, they are not necessarily carbon-free, as the powerplant that generated the electricity to charge the vehicle may have been carbon-emitting. Even when the power to charge the car is coming from a high emission power-source (e.g. a coal power plant), the total carbon emissions is still 60% less than gasoline because internal combustion engines are less efficient and lose much of their energy to heat. When the power for the car comes from a renewable source like wind, solar, or hydro, the net carbon emissions of transportation can drop dramatically to less than 5% of a gasoline-powered car.

In addition, self-driving will enable fewer cars to support our transportation needs. This is because car owners today only use their cars 4-5% of the time. As vehicles become self-driving, each vehicle can be utilized closer to 40-50% of the time through on-demand ride services or vehicle sharing services. If each car is used 10x more, then we could conceivably reduce the number of cars on the road by 70-80%. These changes will lead to cleaner air everywhere and allow us to reexamine the design of cities through reclaiming space currently used for parking.

C. HEAT ENERGY

Industrial Heat

Not all energy we use comes in the form of electricity. In the industrial sector, there are a number of processes where industrial heat is used to create the materials and goods we are all familiar with. Whether it is the smelting and refining of metals like aluminum and iron, creating cement, paper and pulp, or chemical separations from oil and gas refining, there are substantial emissions from the heat energy used in industry. In total it is just a bit smaller than all the emissions for electricity generation (21% vs 25%). To address this, we need to explore new decarbonized production processes. For example, combusting hydrogen to replace coal and natural gas combustion for high temperature smelting. For lower temperature industrial process heat, like industrial steam (used in food and beverage industry to sterilize and cook), we can employ high-lift heat pumps which both improve the energy efficiency and eliminate emissions. For chemical separations, we can develop new molecular sieves and other advanced material science to support low heat sorting technologies.

Home Heat

HVAC in most households is the single largest source of energy use and emissions, constituting more than half of energy use for US homes.[29] Much of that heat comes from natural gas furnaces and boilers which directly drive carbon emissions (and some methane emissions via leaks). In most cases, it is possible to replace these with higher efficiency heat pumps which source ambient heat from the air or ground to reduce the energy needed to heat a home. Such systems can also decrease the cost and improve the efficiency of A/C by applying the same basic idea in reverse.

Thermal Storage

Just as we can use an electric battery to store electric energy and timeshift its use to when it is more needed, we can use thermal storage to do the same with heat energy. For example, during the winter you may store some of the heat directed by your heat pump in the middle of the day (when the smaller difference between outdoor temperature and desired indoor temperature is less leads to better efficiency of operation), and then tap into that stored heat at night to improve the efficiency of heating after the sun goes down. Similarly, since heat pumps are powered by electricity, you may have a system that stores heat at a time of day when electricity prices are lower, and then taps that heat when electricity is more expensive. This same thermal storage technique can also be used for A/C, but instead of storing that heat in concrete or a water tank, the cool (absence of heat, really) is stored in the form of ice or other thermal carrier.

---

[29] https://www.eia.gov/energyexplained/use-of-energy/homes.php

4. MATERIALS

As of 2017, we were averaging 11.5 tons extracted per person per year globally. North America and Europe both came in higher than the average at 30 tons and 20.6 tons per person respectively.[30] In total we are extracting roughly 90B tons of materials per year, 24% by weight are grown materials (agriculture, forestry), 18% are fossil fuels (energy, materials), 10% are metal ores (materials, manufacturing, construction), and the remaining 48% are non-metallic ores (sand and gravel for construction, manufacturing). The total extracted has increased by a factor of three over the last 40 years during a time period where the global population increased by 70% indicating that we are growing our per capita use (by 76% globally) as well as our overall use. While these numbers could be concerning in their own right, the use of material itself does not intrinsically need to be harmful. For example, the grown materials we use could be grown in a soil regenerative manner, leaving the land in better shape than when we began. Thoughtful forest management can lead to vibrant ecosystems while providing substantial forest products including food and timber. We are coming to a better understanding that over millennia, large forest ecosystems from the Amazon[31] to North America[32] to Australia[33] were actually *managed* by native peoples toward the health of forest and community.

That said, when it comes to mined materials such as metals, fossil fuels, sand, and gravel, it's challenging if not impossible for these activities to improve the health of ecosystems. There is a wide range of the damage possible from catastrophic to relatively benign, and over time we need to move toward more recycling of high-value mined materials and lesser and lesser extraction. When we do need to extract, finding lower impact approaches are essential. Specifically, some areas of improvement include 1) reduction, replacement, and capture of acids, solvents, and leaching agents which are part of the mineral extraction, 2) minimizing water use and sharply isolating that wastewater to keep it out of contact with environmental hydrology, and 3) active restoration of disrupted lands.

Ultimately, everything around us is either grown or mined, which makes it clear how much we depend on nature for the lives we lead. The entire economy is either directly connected to material that is grown/mined or manages money and attitudes relative to materials that are grown or mined. Let's dig into more detail to understand how we can evolve in our use of materials.

---

[30] https://www.resourcepanel.org/reports/assessing-global-resource-use

[31] https://www.science.org/doi/full/10.1126/science.aal0157

[32] https://foresthistory.org/education/trees-talk-curriculum/american-prehistory-8000-years-of-forest-management/american-prehistory-essay/

[33] https://www.margulesgroome.com/publications/indigenous-forest-management-in-australia/

A. CLOSING THE LOOP

You may have heard of the concept of "closing the loop" with the materials we use, often used when talking about plastic recycling. At the high level this idea is quite important - the more we can rely on materials we've already mined and the less we can rely on materials that must be newly extracted, the better. In practice, plastics (especially packaging) are one of the worst candidates on this front. We also see this in the outcomes - with 75% of all aluminum ever produced still in circulation because of recycling[34] and 98% of structural steel being recycled into new structural steel.[35] By comparison, only 9% of plastics produced have been successfully recycled.[36] In fact, we have generated as much plastic waste in the 15 years (2005-2020) as we did in all of history leading up to 2005. We have been massively accelerating the waste problem at exactly the point in time when consumers have been most aware of the issue. This speaks to the root, not being one of awareness, but economics.

The key to understanding why some materials work well for closing the loop and others don't is to look at two different attributes: 1) value of material and 2) the level of entropy (disorder) in how it is used. When a material is high value, and its use ends with low disorder, it is a great candidate for closing the loop. We see this in industrial facilities that have metal offcuts which can be easily collected and turned back into new metal, or with industrial solvents that are used to drive a chemical process and are often 95%+ recycled for future work. By comparison, when a material is low value (like most plastics) and the level of disorder is high (e.g. bottles scattered across 1 billion households), then the cost to collect, process, and form new products from the waste will often outstrip the value of the material. This means closing the loop on such materials is intrinsically non-economic and needs to be subsidized. In the case of plastics, it is further worsened by the fact that "plastics" are a label that actually refer to dozens of widely used polymers all with different levels of recyclability and post-consumer value.

Whenever entropy gets high enough, we can look toward Earth-compatible material alternatives. These are often grown materials, as anything that grows is made of materials that Earth and its decomposers intrinsically know how to handle. Given loose and inconsistent labeling standards, a number of materials have been labeled "biodegradable" that still require technical recycling - physical shredding, heating above 100C, special chemical processing, etc. Given that these materials often end up in the environment without going through technical recycling, we prefer the concept of Earth-compatible - which gets to the heart of whether the material creates lasting damage or pollution if left (without special processing) in the environment.

Relative to grown materials, over the millennia we have found a number of plants that provide useful material properties from cotton to hemp to bamboo to rubber trees and much, much more. Grown products are intrinsically Earth-compatible and have many pathways to return gracefully to the environment unless we have treated them with dangerous chemistry or processed them so they do not degrade. There are endless opportunities to take such materials and explore new ways of making use of them for both packaging and for durable products. In addition, we are actively exploring new grown materials from fungi-based materials to bioreactors where we get bacteria or yeast to produce. In terms of what will be an economically viable replacement, one should look at the energy and food inputs required for this type of growing. Traditional grown materials like rubber, hemp or flax have

---

[34] https://international-aluminium.org/resource/aluminium-recycling-fact-sheet/
[35] https://www.aisc.org/why-steel/sustainability/
[36] https://www.science.org/doi/10.1126/sciadv.1700782

the benefit that their energy input comes from the sun. Regional production also helps the economics work out, although if the cost of cleanup was included in the cost of plastic production, many grown materials would already outperform plastics economically.

Lastly, how about the high-value goods with high entropy? As demonstrated with aluminum, if they are easy for consumers to sort and for cities to collect, recycling rates can get into a productive range. When the high value goods are less easy to sort - for example the rare earth and precious metals in an old cell phone or used batteries, then it can be more difficult to collect and to process after the fact. What is needed on this front is to reduce the cost of reverse logistics (the cost of bringing material back from the customer to the manufacturer), and for manufacturers to be transitionally incentivized to reclaim as much valuable material as possible from their post-consumer goods.

With a small bit of investment on these fronts, we reclaim a huge percentage of these high value materials and substantially reduce the upstream need for mining of virgin materials. The idea would be that if it is easy to get the post-consumer goods back to the manufacturer, it would make sense to do slight design changes to their products to make easier to recover the valuable materials – a practice called design for disassembly/ recovery. Afterall, the manufacturing is needing to pay for the cost of virgin material, so if the cost of disassembly and material recovery goes below the cost of new material, over time, more and more materials will be reclaimed from goods as it saves money for the manufacturer. We already see the start of such reverse logistic supply lines around recycling used electric car batteries. A government that would be willing to invest in some reverse logistic infrastructure and apply some temporary incentives around a percentage of post-consumer materials to manufacturers could grow a huge domestic and exportable industry. A more radical proposal that could speed up this transition would be to require any product that is meant to experience its end-of-life with consumers and to be made completely of Earth-compatible materials, and businesses that want to use non-compatible materials be required to structure them as closed-loop service businesses.

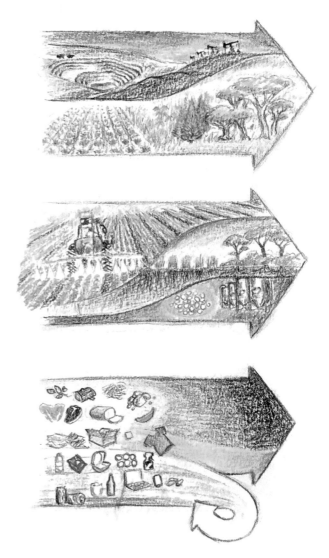

3 Shifts Toward Sustainable Materials:

1) Less mined materials, more grown materials
2) Grown materials produced in soil regenerative ways, or in bioreactors.
3) More Earth-digestible materials, close-looped high-value technical materials.

B. VIEWING OUR CITIES

There is sometimes the impression that city life must be less sustainable as there are so many mined materials and comparatively little nature per acre in the setting. In truth, the material and energy use per capita in cities is lower than that of suburbs. This is easy to see when one considers the plumbing per capita in a 50-unit condo complex vs 50 houses on a suburban street. Many more meters of pipe must be run for the suburb, and this is true for all the other functions and services - wiring, heating/cooling ducts, asphalt, etc. There also tends to be more varied economic opportunities in cities than in rural areas.[37] In 2009, we passed the milestone where worldwide more people are now living in urban areas than rural and since then the concentration continues. This is generally a useful trend for reducing our per capita footprint on nature - especially as we develop and invest in more sustainable cities. The critique that city life is bereft of nature is one we can work on as well. Some studies indicate that more trees in an urban setting improves property values between 10%-32%,[38] a strong motivator for property owners to work with municipal governments to make space for such changes. Additionally, green spaces and green rooftops in urban environments help to combat heat island effect,[39] making cities more enjoyable to live in, resilient to adverse weather events, and potentially saving lives as we anticipate more severe heat waves in the coming decades.

As cities progress in getting more per capita benefit at lower cost for each piece of shared infrastructure, suburbs can use their unique structure to advance other techniques. For example, local generation of power via solar panels, solar hot water heaters, and small-scale wind can all be compelling depending on the specifics of the home. In addition to these changes, heat pumps, smart thermostats, and LED lighting all improve quality of life while saving the homeowner money over time. All of these blend well with an electric vehicle, as it creates a near self-sufficient unit that can be individually resilient and also contribute to grid level resilience.

C. LEARNING FROM NATURE AND SETTING THE BOUNDS

Biomimicry is an approach to learning from nature to help us move toward more effective and more environmentally harmonious solutions to problems we face. It teaches us about the interconnectedness of life and our place in that interconnectedness, since everything in nature has reached a steady state of generation and regeneration through its interconnectedness. It can take the form of direct design inspiration - seed pod barbs designed to stick to fur demonstrating the basic design structure we now use in Velcro,[40] or the microstructure of a butterfly wing meant to capture warmth for the butterfly helping to maximize the capture of sunlight in a solar panel.[41] It can also take the form of more structural ideas - for example, the way that wetlands help to purify waters

---

[37] https://www.un.org/en/development/desa/population/publications/urbanization/urban-rural.asp
[38] https://www.naturewithin.info/Policy/Hedonics_Citations.pdf
[39] https://www.epa.gov/green-infrastructure/reduce-urban-heat-island-effect
[40] Ansberry, Karen, et al. (2020). Nature Did It First: Engineering Through Biomimicry. CA: Dawn Publications.
[41] https://www.theverge.com/2017/10/19/16503258/butterfly-wings-engineering-solar-cell-energy-biomimicry

and contribute to healthy hydrology, or the way a melting snowpack helps to modulate the flow of water over the course of a season.

Biomimicry inspires us to find new ways of creating new ways to live and make products as well as processes, and even policies that may solve our most pressing design challenges sustainably and truly in harmony with all life for better planetary health. We can use biomimicry to heal our world on a personal level as well as on a large scale. With biomimicry we learn from nature's wisdom to heal the planet and ourselves in the process.[42]

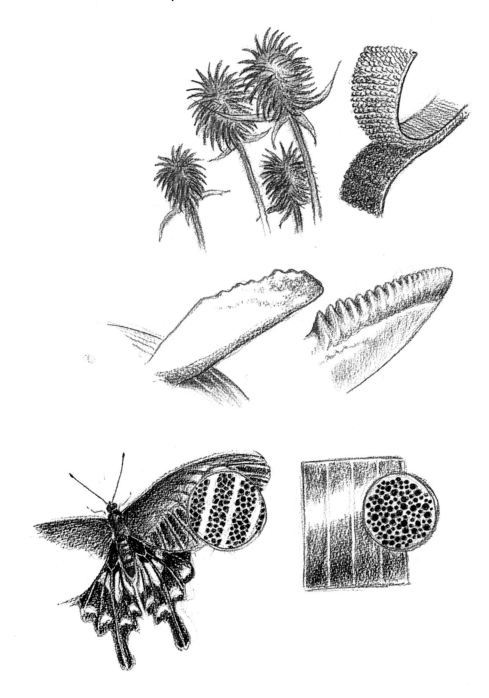

[42] https://biomimicry.org/what-is-biomimicry/

To this end, we might take a moment to explore the larger cycles of material and energy flows in nature and see how it may solve material and energy flows for our society. Everything that has lasted for a long time on this planet is part of cycles of continual generation, reclamation, and renewal. This goes for nutrients, water, and all the physical materials of the planet. Life largely powers this effort either directly from sunlight or recently stored sunlight in the form of chemical energy. Life stores its best ideas in DNA and has built-in a means of adjusting and improving upon those ideas via evolution. Life also adjusts its environment over time with an eye toward supporting more life. For example, healthy soils are created by life, and they hold water for long periods even between droughts, and also retain passages for air exchanges even during times of heavy rain. That access to water and atmosphere allows more life to flourish. Beavers build dams that provide more habitat for fish and birds, and also create areas of land that are resistant to wildfires.[43] Life tends to produce materials that can readily be used by other forms of life, and if there starts to be an overage of any material, nutrient or organism, then new organisms migrate in, or evolve to take advantage of this overabundance.

What one can see from these examples are the beginning of design principles that can teach us all to:
1) Produce and work with Earth-compatible and life-compatible materials
2) Power most of your work via the sun, or sunlight one step removed (wind, hydro, biomass)
3) Encode what works for the planet, not only what is temporarily profitable
4) Address ecosystem imbalances before they build up into damage
5) Have the net output of our efforts create conditions that are net positive to the rest of life.

With these in mind, here are a set of activities we need to
1) Ban forever pollutants and highly toxic chemistry
2) Lean heavily into solar, wind, and energy storage
3) Create substantial penalties for businesses that create long-term ecological damage
4) Use our abilities to monitor ecosystem health to find and address imbalances
5) See the other life on this planet as kin as opposed to being resources.

Pollution takes many forms, but all of them make our environment more dangerous for people and other organisms. The best way to address pollution is to avoid making it in the first place! In situations where this cannot be done, we must capture polluting materials and make them harmless before entering the environment. This can be achieved through filtering, chemistry, biology, and phytoremediation.

The materials that we use fall into two categories -- those that can safely return to the Earth, and those that would be persistently dangerous to the environment. We must work to move toward using materials that easily return to the Earth as much as possible. For the rare occasions that we need to use materials that cannot safely return to the environment, we must make use of them in ways that allow them to be easily reclaimed and out of the waste bin.

This illustration shows some examples of materials that can return to the Earth easily. Pictured here are softwoods, hardwoods, bamboo, rubber trees, jute, organic cotton, hemp, flax, soy and corn:

---

[43] https://www.opb.org/article/2021/11/13/oregon-beaver-conservation-wildlife-science-environment/

5. ENVIRONMENTAL RESTORATION

As mentioned in chapter 4, everything around us is either grown or mined – meaning it comes directly from nature. Given this, we can understand the natural processes that drive the growth of grown things (soil health, access to water, mycelia, beneficial organisms, etc) and the formation of mined things (mineralogical, geological, hydrological processes). Knowing the processes, we can design our economy so that these processes are supported to their maximum capability and then share use of the abundance with all the organisms that benefit from this health.

For example, we have seen in the case of agroforestry in Africa that smallholder farmers have been able to transform land with almost no biomass, featuring caked, cracked earth in the dry season, into land burgeoning with life, providing food, building material, shade, and habitat to their families and many species of plants and animals.[44] They might start with a handful of deep-rooting species and trees that help to bring groundwater up to the surface, then follow it with planting some drought tolerant species (including those that provide food or economic benefit) to cover the land from quickly drying out in the sun. This is then followed by more diversity of beneficial or economic plant species that rely on the improved moisture availability and shade. There are countless practices that teach us how to listen and assess the qualities of land to best understand how to work with land to maximize the ability for life to thrive in that setting. This typically will include an assessment of how to make the most of water resources, sunlight, physical terrain, gravity, etc., and there are frameworks that overlay the social, economic, and cultural elements as well.[45]

Most approaches show marked improvement to land quality within 2 to 3 years, and many can realize total transformation within 5 to 10 years.

Outside of any specific technique, it should be understood that at the high level the life-supporting capability of the landscape is being increased and humans are benefitting from taking a comparatively small slice of the natural wealth being created. This leaves plenty for the other organisms that have all contributed to the health of the landscape, and creates a landscape that can produce as much or more the following year with less effort. This would be a wonderful gift to the land and to future generations.

Compare this approach and mindset to the typical short-term return, industrial mindset. This mindset would see an already healthy ecosystem, say a forest, and see it as a "natural resource" to be extracted and converted into board-feet for the lumber industry or pulp for the paper industry. Governments, which are meant to operate outside of the quick-turn commercial cycle and think

---

[44] https://www.sciencedirect.com/science/article/pii/S1877343513001449

[45] http://www.regrarians.org/regrarians-handbook/

about the longer term health of the collective commons, are often the broker selling off access to extract these resources to the highest bidder.

Part of this is rooted in a wrong understanding of such land as static resources as opposed to dynamic landscapes where a small investment in the foundational metabolic processes creating natural wealth yields massive benefits that quickly outpace the value of rapid extraction. Certainly, better policies focused on building natural capital would help, but more conscious leadership can lead the way here by starting these practices now, thereby simplifying the process of policy that further supports the work. While historically it has always been more "profitable" to treat natural resources in this way, in a world of intensifying climate destabilization, it will be the businesses that are adopting these stabilizing, long-term focused practices that thrive. With this frame in mind, let's explore a new relationship to the planet.

A. FORESTS

Global forests constitute roughly 3 trillion trees and currently cover roughly one quarter of all land on the planet. Human activity has been steadily decreasing global forest coverage since the start of agriculture 12,000 years ago, with our current estimates that roughly 46% of global forest cover has been lost since then.[46] We currently lose a net of 6 billion trees per year, and while deforestation rates have come down somewhat in the last two decades, we continue to be reducing forest cover and degrading forest quality at large scale. What would it look like to get on the other side of this dynamic to be a civilization that is restoring forest cover and deepening forest quality around the world? What if we were so effective at this that we still had all the timber, paper, and pulp we need?

First, we need to examine how forests grow larger and healthier. For a forest to grow larger, it needs to take up more area, and the interesting zone is the current boundary between forest and an adjacent landscape such as shrubland or mixed grassland. At this boundary, seed dispersal, supported by both abiotic (wind, water) and biotic (birds, rodents) processes, help to expand forests by carrying those seeds into this new area. Given this, forests tend to grow to immediately adjacent areas, and given the massive scale of our historical deforestation, it may take thousands of years for forests to propagate across the landscape back to the historical range that is capable of sustaining forests. This is a place for both people and technology to assist by speeding up the process with thoughtful seed dispersal. People can identify degraded lands that were once forested and make plans to either hand-plant, or deploy machines such as tree-planting and seed-dispersing drones to get a diverse set of seeds that are appropriate for the landscape planted in a shorter amount of time without the need of being immediately adjacent to existing forests. Earth-moving machines may also be deployed to create berms, swales, terraces, and other features to help improve residency time of water until enough plants and healthy soils can take up the task.

Because of advancements in robotic planting and machine vision for ecosystem monitoring, the cost of restoration per hectare is coming down exponentially, which means it will become economical

---

[46] https://www.nature.com/articles/nature.2015.18287

to restore more degraded land for the dollar. Beyond the benefits to the immediate surroundings, it turns out there are far-reaching impacts to restoring forests. It is now becoming better understood that forests not only benefit from rains, but via transpiration, cloud seeding, and atmospheric pressure differences that forests generate, they actually create the rains as well.[47] Large-scale patterns of forestation can change atmospheric hydrology at a continental scale,[48] meaning that a thoughtful approach to reforestation can help to stabilize climate and improve resilience at a scale that improves conditions thousands of miles away.

[47] https://www.inderscienceonline.com/doi/abs/10.1504/IJW.2010.038729

[48] https://iopscience.iop.org/article/10.1088/1748-9326/aaba0f/pdf

B. GRASSLANDS

Much of the world's grasslands and shrublands have already been annexed by industry for cattle grazing. Unfortunately, such grazing has been done in a way that degrades the soils and landscape, as cattle are left to graze land until much of the biomass is gone - making it more vulnerable to flood and drought, and generally making it more difficult for the land to recover. Other historical grasslands have been converted to industrial farmlands, replacing large biodiverse swaths with monocultures that require mass amounts of fertilizer, pesticides, herbicides. All the while, a shockingly low percentage of this food is used to directly feed people (21% in the case of US corn).[49] This is true of most industrially-produced crops and it counters the narrative from the big agriculture companies that high-input industrial practices are key because they "feed the world." Provably, they contribute the minority of food calories, while capturing most of the profit of the farming industry.[50] The 79% is going to animal feed and biofuels, where only about 4% of the caloric energy we feed to animals makes it to humans for consumption.

As we invest in new approaches to agriculture, as described in Chapter 2, we will be able to increase farm profitability while needing vastly less land to grow our food. Alternative protein production will radically reduce the need for animal feed and the land associated with growing that feed. This will create an opportunity for us to do mass restoration of these landscapes to rebuild ecosystems and soil on land degraded by industrial agriculture and overgrazing. We can already start now on land we are managing for agriculture, via planting of deep-rooted perennials, the addition of pollinator strips, diverse cover cropping to restore soil nutrients, and intensive rotational grazing to improve the soil microbiome.

As we take a step back from these lands and allow nature to do more of the work, we can create landscapes that rebuild our base of pollinators and beneficial insect species, return birds and mammals to the landscape, and even explore the reintroduction of large grazers like bison. These landscapes can continue to be economically useful as they restore, as we can harvest hay for feed and insulation, intersperse fiber crops for materials, switchgrass for biofuels, while growing livestock in an ecologically sound way. These are different management practices, for sure, but they are ones with huge potential to be more profitable to farmers and improve their profitability over time as soil and landscape recover.

Much of this discussion has been focused around the economics of agriculture, as farmers and ranchers currently manage much of the grassland on the planet. In the longer run though, we can imagine large restored swaths that are largely managed by nature, via the actions of animals and plants in the landscape, providing safe passage for migrating species and returning biodiversity.

---

[49] https://www.usda.gov/sites/default/files/documents/coexistence-corn-factsheet.pdf
[50] https://cropwatch.unl.edu/tightening-your-belt-refocusing-profitability

C. WETLANDS

The wetlands of the world, whether they be swamps, marshes, mangroves, or bogs are often seen as less desirable because they are more difficult to build on, are hard to traverse, and are home to mosquitoes. Defined as land which is constantly or often covered by water, they provide essential ecosystem services such as cleaning water before it reaches the sea, modulating floodwaters, processing decaying matter, managing sediment, and providing essential habitat to fish, birds, and other wildlife. Pertinent to our current overage of CO_2 in the atmosphere, wetlands have tremendous carbon storage because of their consistent coverage by slow-moving or stagnant waters.[51] Specifically, the water coverage drives anoxic decomposition - decay in the absence of oxygen, which tends to store the carbon in the decaying matter in the soil instead of releasing the carbon as CO_2 during the decay process. The result is soils that can contain 12-18% soil organic carbon,[52] roughly 10 times more than most soils. Wetlands concentrate a lot of ecological benefits in a small area making them very valuable to restore per acre.

One potential means to economically pursue their restoration is based on their benefits for water treatment and water quality. Well-placed wetlands reduce the cost of water treatment, and since this is an ongoing benefit for an upfront restoration effort, there's the possibility of financing this work via the cost reduction. There are also benefits for flood protection and resilience, which may appeal to insurance companies to address and thereby reduce the potential for water damaged property and large insurance payouts when severe weather reaches a region. Coastal wetlands like mangroves can be good grounds for fishing and when managed well, provide food and materials to local communities. These are also places of great natural beauty and biodiversity. Organizing environmentally respectful tourism activities like walks, plein air painting and photography sessions, meditation classes, and communing with nature for psychological restoration are just a few examples of how to appreciate the beauty in our natural surroundings more.

D. OCEANS

The oceans are currently beset by numerous threats, ranging from pollution (effluent, fertilizer, oil spills, plastics, noise), to habitat destruction (reefs, wetlands, seafloor trawling, coastal erosion), to damaging fishing practices, to macro threats like thermal stress, upwelling suppression, and acidification. We are currently on a course where all of the world's reefs will be under severe threat by 2050 with the complete extinction of corals from the planet following within a few decades.[53] This loss alone will extinct at least 25% of all ocean species.

The surface of the ocean is in broad contact with the Earth's atmosphere, and it has absorbed roughly ¼ of the carbon we've released in the atmosphere. This has been incredibly helpful, but it has also led to the oceans worldwide becoming 30% more acidic. If we succeed in bringing down

---

[51] https://www.nature.com/articles/ncomms13835
[52] https://www.britannica.com/science/Histosol-soil
[53] https://files.wri.org/d8/s3fs-public/pdf/reefs_at_risk_revisited_executive_summary.pdf

our emissions, and then advance to absorbing our historical excesses into plants and soils, the ocean will begin to release the carbon it has captured and de-acidify. The goal is through these actions, for us to return the Earth's carbon concentration to what it was before the start of the industrial revolution. However, if we allow the oceans to continue acidifying, it becomes more difficult for shelled organisms to form their shells and losing shelled organisms would lead to a collapse of numerous marine ecosystems around the world.[54] In short, we are at a critical passage for the future of the oceans and we are facing many forms of irreversible damage stemming from a mass extinction we've initiated.

Given that we have created the situation, we are also in a great position to chart a new course. With that in mind, there are many ways for us to repair the damage and get the oceans on a trajectory for long term health, which in turn will support our long-term health.

1) Farming with less fertilizer runoff is both more cost effective and prevents algae blooms and oxygen dead zones.
2) Better management of industrial and human effluent and effective water treatment in concert with wetland restoration can address much of the chemical pollution making it into the ocean.
3) We are already on a trajectory where aquaculture (fish grown in controlled environments) represents almost half of total production – 82 million tons in 2018 compared to caught fish representing 96 million tons.[55] Continuing this trend while finding more sustainable ways to produce fish feed and manage fish waste could dramatically reduce fishing pressures
4) Active protection and restoration of the most sensitive biodiverse regions, including coral reefs, sea grasses, and mangroves, while we push on the larger work to eliminate greenhouse gas emissions and establish large scale sequestration.
5) Returning whales to their pre-industrial populations could drive 1.7 billion tons of CO2 sequestration / year.[56] We could do this by incentivizing reduction of ship strikes and a reduction of whale-disorienting military sonar.[57]

As ocean losses have mounted, we have deepened our ability to monitor ocean ecosystems via satellite and with drone surveying we can apply that technology to monitor critical ecosystems and track key populations, like large whales. We are also beginning to build active interventions, such as coral spawning/planting robots and sea-grass planting robots. With these incredible new technologies there is newfound hope for ocean life. We're also exploring marine permaculture arrays that could support the revival of seaweed and kelp forests. These activities may be economically supported by their value for coastal protection, especially during an era of increased storm activity and stronger hurricanes. They could also be economically valuable for their role in improving the productivity of fisheries and mariculture. Lastly, as we better understand the carbon flux of various marine ecosystems, they may be supported by net-zero carbon sequestration programs.

---

[54] https://www.whoi.edu/multimedia/carbon-dioxide-shell-building-and-ocean-acidification/
[55] https://www.fao.org/state-of-fisheries-aquaculture
[56] https://www.imf.org/external/pubs/ft/fandd/2019/12/natures-solution-to-climate-change-chami.htm
[57] https://oceanconference.un.org/commitments/?id=21408

There is hope for our oceans. To prevent further damage, we need to only use reef safe sunscreen, limit upstream sources of pollution, and protect key areas from damaging fishing practices or excess tourism. Let's learn how to protect, heal, and regenerate ocean ecosystems. We can be the civilization that re-plants and tends the reefs to help them through a few generations while we work to get the planetary temperature stabilized. With some extra care and commitment, we can ensure that future generations can also cherish our beautiful coral reefs. Give what you can and perhaps volunteer with some of the wonderful organizations protecting our oceans. You can also adopt coral through an organization like Coral Vita.[58] Coral Vita has discovered a way to grow climate change resilient coral up to fifty times faster to help regenerate dying reefs.[59]

E. BIODIVERSITY

The planet's biodiversity is a gift we have inherited, and we will strive to pass it on to future generations. There is amazing beauty and diversity enriching every corner of the globe, and as we work to restore the natural habitat of our plants and animals we can flourish alongside nature and the growing richness of our planet. Learn about endangered species and ways to help wildlife. Think of ideas to help share the beauty of nature and it's genius ways of creating, regenerating, adapting, growing, and healing.

[58] https://www.coralvita.co/
[59] https://www.instagram.com/coralvitareefs/

6. REFLECTION & CLOSING

Sometimes it is valuable to step back from the day-to-day ways of thinking - work, family, community, education, entertainment, games and other media to understand some of the fundamental truths. It's worth remembering that what we have on this planet is extremely *rare*. While there are many stars in the universe and many planets around those stars, few planets exist in the zone where liquid water and carbon-based life can form. Even our planet, which has been incredibly fortunate, has had multicellular life for less than 20% of its existence. Humans have existed for a few million years and culture for tens of thousands. Modern engineering got going a few hundred years ago. These skills have allowed us to make tools to peer into the stars, date the fossil record, and make sense of our place in the grand sweep of universal history.

While we will always have the immediate challenges of work, health, government, social injustice, and living through challenging times it is helpful to remember that life is a miracle worth cherishing. Part of healing the planet begins with healing ourselves, and this can start by simply taking a deep breath and feeling the life-giving oxygen from nature flowing through you and as you breathe out, letting go of any tension. Remember to practice self-care and self-appreciation and it is helpful to remember how much we've created and how powerful our capacity to create can be when applied to the long-term health of humanity and nature. In addition, at times it's helpful to reground in this larger context, examine any activity happening in industry or policy, and ask the question: *What would happen if we were to continue it for 1000 years?* Over that time period, minor ills of a practice can add up, and destabilizing directions end quite quickly. On the flip side, over 1000 years, minor positives can add up to profound natural wealth for many generations to come. This thought process gets us out of the short-term mindset and also asks us to consider what metabolic flows of nature are affected as a practice continues.

Λ. SEEKING A NET POSITIVE FUTURE

- *Why are we here?*
- *What kind of world can we create?*

With these questions in mind, we can see why it is important for our civilization as a whole to move toward becoming a net positive to nature. Even if each year led to the accumulation of a tiny bit of damage - say 0.1% of nature was seriously damaged per year - it would spell the end of civilization within 1000 years. At the moment we are doing more than 0.1% damage, which is why the warnings have been so grave and the damage adding up around us has been so acute. But this damage is not inherent to what we are, it is a result of design choices – in what we've chosen to make and how, in what we encourage and discourage in our society, and the choice of whose voices are included in the process of creating our shared future.

As we've discussed in this writing, we are perfectly capable of adding to the health of the natural systems that support us and benefiting ourselves tremendously while taking care of the rest of life and future generations. There is one sense of the future which is about frontiers – the expansion of what is possible, but there is another sense of the future which is about harmony– that our societies can progress from being less kind to being more kind, that people of different backgrounds can come from less understanding toward having more understanding. That our standard of living can improve while not limiting the standard of living of all other life around us.

While there are many calls to cut emissions to avoid disaster at the moment, and it is factually true that we must dramatically reduce or eliminate emissions entirely, avoiding disaster is not anyone's vision of an inspiring goal. Who wants to strive for a world that is just a shade above disaster? This is why, even if it takes longer - and truly, it could take 1000 years - we need to set our sights on the larger goal of becoming net positive to nature and to each other. It's truly worth working toward and looking at our societal and personal decisions through that lens will teach us so much about our potential as a species.

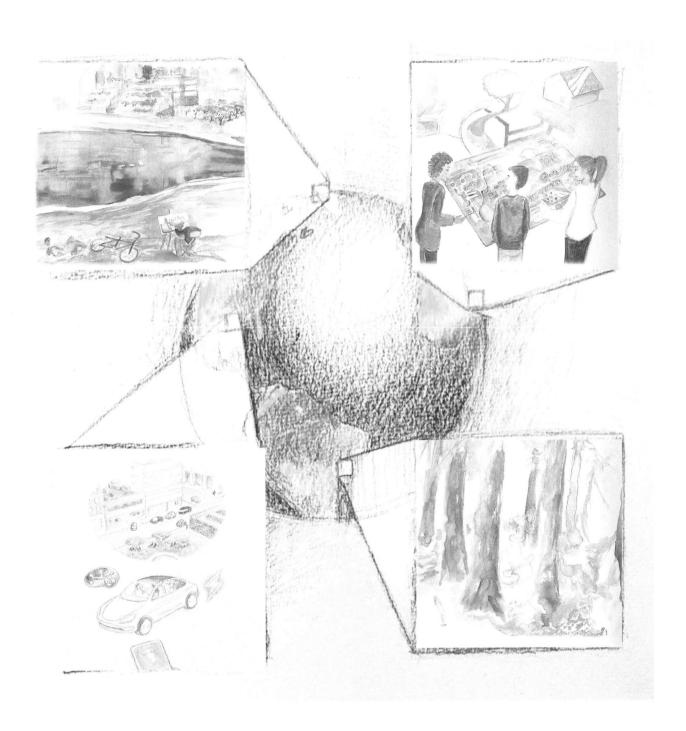

B. ALL TOGETHER

What does it look like for all humanity and all of life to begin working together?

1) We seek to learn from the widest base of lived experiences and have compassion for those experiences. This means the inclusion of many voices including those not traditionally in power as a means of really hearing what work needs to be done to care for each other.

2) Each level of action seeks to maximize diverse nutrient flows. The algorithm of life on this planet is to encode abilities and metabolisms that over time maximize diverse nutrient flows. Or, as Biomimicry author Janine Benyus likes to say, "life creates the conditions for more life."[60] When we maximize diverse nutrient flows, it means we are always looking for how to support more life in the actions we take, the way we design our tools, our society and more. With this knowledge in mind let's consider new genius ideas that do just that.

3) Collective resources are brought together to invest in infrastructure that respects nature while reducing the cost of accessing key services. When a permaculture expert builds berms and swales to move moisture across a landscape, they are creating infrastructure for life. We need to invest in infrastructure that makes access to water, healthy food, clean air, and productive waste processing as inexpensive as possible. A healthy ecosystem does the same for the life that takes part in it - it lowers the cost of access to all these same services.

4) Beyond physical infrastructure, humans must invest in the infrastructure of compassion and understanding. What are the tools that support quality understanding, collective care, rest and recreation, and the pursuit of purpose? Let us refine those tools with each generation and pass on this wealth in the form of a healthier society in each generation.

5) We must remember our common origins and care for our collective future. A person gets roughly half their DNA from each of their two parents, and roughly a quarter from each grandparent. With each generation doubling the number of people that contributed to our existence, it means that just 10 generations back (roughly 250 years) we came from 1024 people and 20 generations back (500 years) we came from close to 1 million people. We are all more closely connected than we recognize, and our future together is deeply intertwined. To treat each other as separate locked in the "rat race" or "survival of the fittest" is a recent game we invented that has some useful attributes in accelerating a market economy, but hollows out the truth of who we really are.

6) Our relationships can be infinite wells. With the people we are the closest, we are able to share and see so much nuance, to develop so much beauty and complexity in how we relate. This is true between people, it is true of people and their pets, we've seen it to be true between animals even across different species. When we remember how much beauty we can create from this depth and nuance, it helps us resist the commodification of self and other that we so often advance when we think only of markets. These infinite wells show the potential of what all of us can be. Simply carving out time daily to do some deep breathing in nature and meditating on the magic of the universe does wonders for our entire being. Let's dare to dream of a better future together. One that especially honors the intricate harmony of the natural world around us.

---

[60] Benyus, Janine M. (2002). Biomimicry: Innovation Inspired by Nature. NY: HarperCollins.

By employing the ideas above, we believe we can approach the next chapter of our journey as a species together with so much more clarity, truth, and excitement in shared possibility. As Buddhist author Thich Nhat Hahn has explained, we and everything we encounter is miraculously connected through a web of interbeing: "If you are a poet, you will see clearly that there is a cloud floating in this sheet of paper. Without a cloud, there will be no rain; without rain, the trees cannot grow; and without trees, we cannot make paper. The cloud is essential for the paper to exist. If the cloud is not here, the sheet of paper cannot be here either."[61]

With a more integrated understanding of planetary health and a compassionate and creative lens toward the ways we can build the future together, we can have society itself become an act of planetary healing. So let's learn, explore, and build together, listen together, reflect together, and dream big with such possibility in mind. Let's think practically about the future and the genius ideas for planetary healing waiting to be born and nurtured. We can begin by spending more time appreciating the natural world. That time spent will help us be attuned to nature in a state of health and better understand when our actions lessen that health. Also, the gratitude and awe we experience in our interactions with nature provide us with the lived understanding that life is interwoven in cycles of giving and receiving. Even a simple snack of strawberries and honey connect us to the effort of the bees, flowers, clouds, and sun. Let's align with the natural gifts we've been given as a species to better perceive, appreciate, and become a friend of the natural world.

When we meditate in nature we can immerse ourselves in the elemental properties of the planet (such as water, rain, sun, the many plants and trees, all the incredible species, wind, and earth), we experience a deep understanding and reverence as well as intense gratitude for life and the regenerative energies of nature here on our amazing planet Earth.[62] When we take the time to truly feel the healing peace of the natural world and practice breathing in nature while appreciating the oxygen our green spaces provide, we allow nature to soothe and heal us in a way where we not only feel inspired, but, we're also better able to reawaken our incredible abilities to understand and communicate with the natural world. We realize that not only do we breathe in gifts from nature via the oxygen in each breath, we give back to nature with our existence, and we can build our world in a way that preserves this foundational reality.

Let's bring plants into our lives and homes so we can consistently experience this life-giving exchange. Let's volunteer a weekend to plant trees and native species or get involved in supporting an endangered species you connect with. In our lives, one personal example of this realization is our passion for saving the coral reefs. We began by spending time exploring tide pools that had been brimming with colorful underwater creatures and filled with a rainbow of coral, now bleached and gone. This has led to feeling this loss deeply and drove us to conceptualize a coral-planting robot that can scalably restore marine life ecosystems. This is just one of many ideas that we can all dream, develop, and find ways to support on the expanding horizon of new technological ideas that will help to heal the planet. We are excited to think of and learn about new inventions that will restore our oceans and sustain ocean life.

---

[61] https://www.awakin.org/v2/read/view.php?tid=222
[62] Lee, Ilchi, et al. (2010). Nature Heals: Meditations for Self-Healing (Audible Audiobook – Unabridged). AZ: BEST Life Media.

C. MEDITATIONS FOR PLANETARY HEALING

Let's meditate. Take some big deep healing breaths and meditate on the planet and all the amazing beings that inhabit it. Imagining this lovely, new and exciting future geared towards being a restorative force on the planet by creating and healing together. Use your imagination to envision a better world and ask what your life would look like with healthier habits, time in nature, space for connection and reflection. Imagine the most beautiful place in nature you've ever seen. Perhaps there are landscapes you've dreamed of, like waterfalls and bubbling streams with colorful sparkling stones and playful fish, mountains, beautiful trees, flowers and birds of all kinds. Our personal dreams help to expand and shape our collective dreams and lead to care and consideration that can return our planet to vibrant health.

Together, by breathing deeply and rhythmically, paying attention to all the areas of our bodies that our breath sends oxygen to, and imaging the healing powers of the natural world, we can work to heighten our consciousness of our powerful ability to heal both ourselves and the planet at large.

Let's continue to envision a world where the presence of humanity benefits nature in the same way nature nourishes us, truly giving back knowing that such gifts create bounty for ourselves and future generations. Imagine enough food, shelter, and energy for all and the many ways of working together to make things better for all. Let's make our practices net positive to nature. Shaping our businesses so things are better for all involved. Shaping the future with positive handprints[63] of change that involve improving lives and planetary well-being.

With each new step forward in the direction of sustainability we can imagine a world together that values improving the quality of life here on Earth for everyone, honoring peace, kindness to one another and respect for future generations. Let's breathe this understanding into every cell of our bodies as love shapes and guides our actions.

While deep in meditation it is helpful to continuously ask the question - *how will humanity through its relationships and capabilities foster the flourishing of the natural world?*

Imagine your ideal place in nature to explore and recharge. Perhaps you're creating one with your imagination and that's wonderful. There are so many amazing places filled with wonder on this planet. Let your mind be as free as a bird as you soar through the ideas that will help with planetary healing.

As we heal, the world heals, as we shift, the world around us shifts, we are powerful creators and can do anything with our minds. Let's make up our minds to save our home here on Earth and to do so with love and compassion. Let's help the endangered species survive, to regenerate places that have been destroyed and work with planetary cycles to make this world a better place. Let's think of ideas for our future steps of change towards sustainability and let's share this greater consciousness of what it takes to sustain life with everyone willing to learn and grow. We are nature and it is within us to find a way.[64]

---

[63] Polman, Paul, and Winston, Andrew. S. (2021). Net Positive: How Courageous Companies Thrive by Giving More Than They Take. MA: Harvard Business Review Press.

[64] http://www.ourprosperousplanet.com/meditations/genius_meditations_1.mp3 and http://www.ourprosperousplanet.com/meditations/genius_meditations_2.mp3

7. FURTHER READING:

Ansberry, Karen, et al. (2020). Nature Did It First: Encourage Problem-Solving and Exploration Through Nature with a Science Book for Kids About Biomimicry and Engineering. CA: Dawn Publications.

Benyus, Janine M. (2002). Biomimicry: Innovation Inspired by Nature. NY: HarperCollins.

Bucke, Richard M. (1991 - *Republished from 1901*). Cosmic Consciousness: A Study in the Evolution of the Human Mind. London, UK: Penguin.

Flach, Tim, et al. (2017). Endangered. NY: Abrams.

Hanh, Thich Nhat (2021). Zen and the Art of Saving the Planet. NY: HarperOne.

Hawken, Paul (2021). Regeneration: Ending the Climate Crisis in One Generation. London, UK: Penguin Books.

Herzog, Howard J. (2018). Carbon Capture (The MIT Press Essential Knowledge series). Cambridge, MA: The Mit Press.

Lee, Ilchi, et al. (2010). Nature Heals: Meditations for Self-Healing (Audible Audiobook – Unabridged). AZ: BEST Life Media (Publisher).

Lovins, Hunter L. (2018). A Finer Future: Creating an Economy in Service to Life. Gabriola, BC: New Society Publishers.

Manahan, Stanley (2011). Green Chemistry and the Ten Commandments of Sustainability, Third Edition. Columbia, MO: ChemChar Research.

Pearce, Fred. (2021). A Trillion Trees. How We Can Reforest Our World. Croydon, UK: Granta Publishing

Polman, Paul, and Winston, Andrew. S. (2021). Net Positive: How Courageous Companies Thrive by Giving More Than They Take. MA: Harvard Business Review Press.

Smith, Katy, et al. (2005). The New Atlas of Planet Management. Berkeley, CA: University of California Press.

Stika, Jon, et al. (2016). A Soil Owner's Manual: How to Restore and Maintain Soil Health. CA: CreateSpace Independent Publishing Platform.

NOTES

NOTES

NOTES

NOTES

NOTES

NOTES

NOTES

NOTES

Printed in the United States
by Baker & Taylor Publisher Services